All Tied Up

Written by Claire Owen

Peru

My name is Rosa. I live in the city of Lima, Peru. At school, my favorite subject is math. Without using pencil and paper, how could you record numbers? Can you think of any ways people have done this in the past?

Contents

Wherever you
see me, you'll find
activities to try and
questions to answer.

The Inca Empire

A South American Indian people called the *Inca* once
ruled the largest and richest empire in all of the Americas.
In the 1200s, the Inca began building cities and roads
in the area that is now Peru. By 1438, the Inca empire
stretched for 2,500 miles along the west coast of South
America. It had become a highly
developed civilization.

empire   a group of countries or regions under the control of one
         government or ruler

SOUTH
AMERICA

THE INCA EMPIRE

Inca stonemasons could fit stones together so closely that it is impossible to insert a thin knife blade between the stones.

Inca Roads

The Inca capital was Cuzco. In the Quechua language of the Inca, the name *Cuzco* means "the navel of the world." The city had many stone buildings and palaces, and temples richly decorated with gold and silver. About 125,000 people lived in or near Cuzco. Two main roads ran north and south, connected to every village by smaller roads and hanging bridges. The total length of Inca roadways was more than 14,000 miles.

The Inca traveled mostly by walking. Llamas were used to carry heavy loads. Today in Peru, many Quechua people still follow traditional ways of life.

About how far from Cuzco is Quito? How many miles from Quito is Santiago? (Use the scale on the map to help estimate each distance.)

The Inca Road Network
Scale: 1 inch = 300 miles

Quito

SOUTH AMERICA

Cuzco

Santiago

The Inca used cables of braided grass to build bridges over rivers and gorges.

Relay Runners

To govern their huge empire, the Inca needed a good system of communication. They set up relay stations along the roads, about $1\frac{1}{2}$ miles apart. At these stations, runners waited to carry messages. As a runner approached a station, he blew into a conch shell to warn the next runner to get ready. Using this system, a message could be carried as far as 150 miles in a single day.

communicate   to exchange, or pass along, information

Today, a good runner can run $1\frac{1}{2}$ miles in about 10 minutes. About how many hours would a relay of such runners take to cover 150 miles?

The distance from Cuzco to Quito is about 1,200 miles. About how many days would it take to send a message from Cuzco to Quito?

Keeping Count

The Inca were very organized. Officials were in charge of keeping records, ordering supplies, and collecting taxes from the people. However, the Inca had not developed any written language, so they had no way of writing numbers. Instead, they used a cord with knotted strings known as a *quipu* (kee pooh) to record numbers. In the Quechua language, the word *quipu* means "knot."

This old drawing shows an official (right) using a quipu to present a report to a nobleman (left).

Did You Know?

Some people believe that quipu may also have been used to store songs, poems, calendar information, and even laws.

The Inca officials who made and read quipu were called *quipucamayocs*. Today in Peru, modern-day quipu makers keep the ancient art alive.

Tying the Knots

Each string on a quipu showed one number. To show 734, for example, a quipu maker would tie 7 single knots close together, toward the top of the string. These knots would show the hundreds. Farther down the string, the quipu maker would tie 3 knots to show the tens. At the end of the string, he would tie a long knot with 4 loops (like example *B* below) to show the ones.

Decoding the Knots

Single knots were used to show tens, hundreds, and so on.	In the ones place, long knots showed 2 ones to 9 ones.	In the ones place, a figure-eight knot showed a single one.
A 	**B** 	**C** 
To show 3 tens, for example, three single knots were tied in the tens place.	The long knot above has four loops, so it shows 4 ones.	There was no knot for zero.

The total of several numbers was shown on an extra string at the right. This string was threaded through the other strings.

Which of the strings above shows the number 250? What do the other strings show? Which string shows the sum of the other three numbers?

All Tied Up

Quipu strings were made from colored cotton or llama wool. Their light weight made them easy for a messenger to carry. The colors of the strings, the way the strings were connected, and the spaces between the strings all had special meanings. Quipu could only be made and understood by experts who had special training.

Most quipu were destroyed at the end of the Inca empire. Today, only a few hundred Inca quipu remain in museums around the world.

Figure It Out

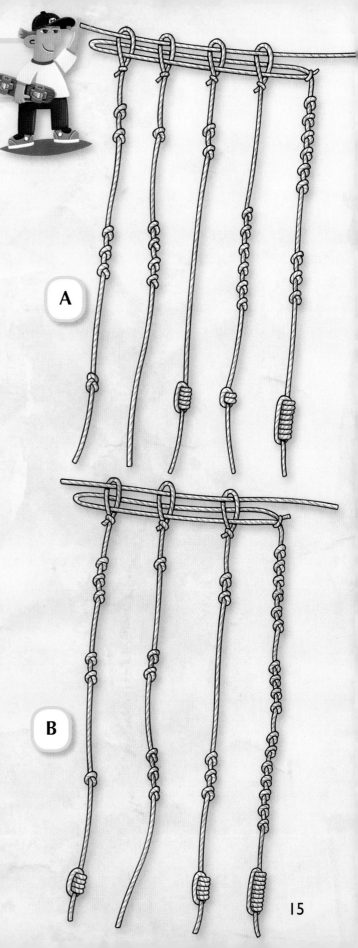

1. Answer these questions for quipu A. Then answer them again for quipu B.

   a. How many numbers are shown on the quipu?

   b. How many places are shown on the strings of the quipu?

   c. What numbers do the quipu show?

   d. Does the "total" string on the right show the correct number?

A

2. Why didn't the Inca need a knot to show zero?

3. Make or draw each of the following:

   a. a three-string quipu that shows 316; 263; and 108

   b. a two-string quipu that shows 4,112 and 3,536

   Now add an extra string to each quipu and use it to show the total.

B

Recording a Census

When the results of a population census were recorded on a quipu, the first string at the left showed the number of people over the age of 60. The next six strings recorded people 51 to 60 years old, 41 to 50 years old, and so on. The eighth string showed the number of babies less than a year old. Men and women were counted on separate quipus.

Pretend that this quipu shows census results for the women of an Inca village. How many women were aged 31 to 40? What else does the quipu show?

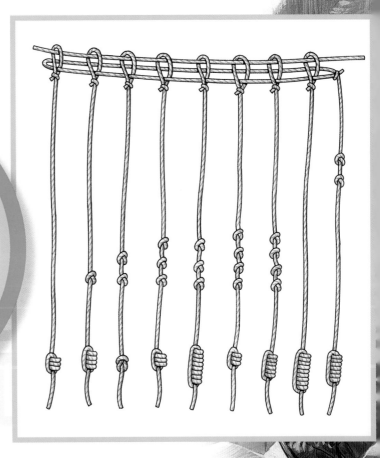

census   an official count of how many people live in a country or an area

Make a Quipu

You will need up to nine cords or strings.
Ask your teacher or principal how many children
there are in each grade level at your school.

1. Tie one of the cords across a desk or the back of a chair. This is the main cord.

2. Tie knots on a cord to show the total number of children in kindergarten at your school. Tie this cord to the main cord.

(You may use single knots for the ones, if you wish.)

3. Repeat step 2 for grade 1, grade 2, and so on.

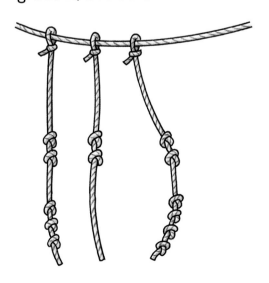

4. Now calculate the total number of children at your school. Add an extra cord to show that number.

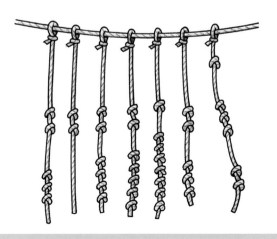

The Incan "Abacus"

The Inca used the quipu as a data storage system. When they needed to make calculations, however, they used a counting board called a *yupana*. The simplest yupana was a grid drawn in the dirt. Numbers were represented by placing corn kernels on the grid. The value of each kernel depended on both the row and the column on the grid.

This picture is from a long letter to the king of Spain that was written in 1615. In the bottom left-hand corner is a yupana with the maximum number of corn kernels in each square.

calculate   to figure out

Yupana Counting Board

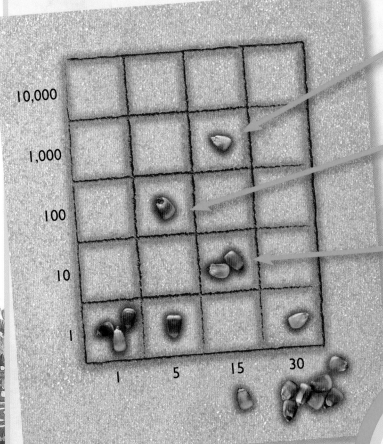

10,000

1,000

100

10

1

1   5   15   30

This corn kernel represents 15,000.

This corn kernel shows 500.

Each of these kernels represents 15 tens, or 150.

What is the total value of the corn kernels on the yupana above? Pick two of those kernels. If you remove them, what is the new total value?

Several museums have stone yupanas from Peru, like this one. No one is sure exactly how they were used.

The End of an Empire

At its height, the Inca empire had a population of about 6 million. The empire came to an end in 1532 when Spanish conquistadors reached South America. By 1561, three-fourths of the native people had died, most of them from smallpox, measles, and influenza. These diseases were unknown in the Americas before the arrival of the Europeans.

The European invaders looted the Inca cities and melted down most of the gold they found.

Santo Domingo

The temples of the Inca were destroyed. In some cities, the Spanish built churches on top of the walls of the old temples.

conquistadors   soldiers who conquered Mexico and Peru in the 16th century

How many native people died in the 30 years from 1532 to 1561? About how many deaths is that each year? … each month? … each day?

Today, the ruins of a fortress near Cuzco (top) and the "lost city" of Machu Picchu (above) help to keep the memory of the Inca empire alive.

American Numbers

Throughout the Americas, different native peoples spoke different languages and developed their own number systems. Many of those number systems were similar to that of the Inca, in that they were based on 10. In Central America and in the far north, however, number systems were based on 20. On the west coast, some people used systems based on 2, 4, 8, 16, or a combination of those numbers.

The Yuki people of northern California used the spaces between their fingers to help them count. They had names for numbers to 16 and combined those names to make other numbers.

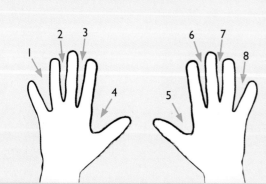

The Aztec used four picture symbols to show numbers. To show 60, for example, they would draw the symbol for 20 three times.

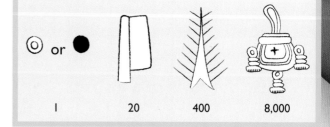

The traditional oral counting system of the Alaskan Inuit was based on 20. In 1994, some students invented symbols to represent the counting numbers. This system is now being used in many of the local schools.

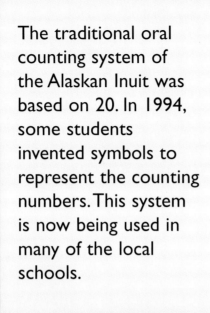

NORTH
AMERICA

The Maya of Central America had symbols for the numbers 0 to 19.

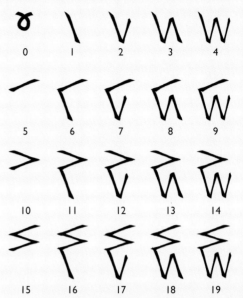

SOUTH
AMERICA

Sample Answers

> Find out about a number system from another part of the world. For example, you could investigate the numerals used by the Babylonians, Egyptians, Chinese, or Romans.

Page 7   about 1,200 miles;
about 2,500 miles

Page 9   about 8 days;
about 17 hours (1,000 minutes)

Page 13   the second string from the left;
146; 42; 438
the string at the right

Page 15
1. Quipu A: a. 5   b. 3
   c. 231; 140; 205; 62, 638
   d. Yes
   Quipu B: a. 4   b. 4
   c. 3,214; 1,230; 2,035;
   6,479   d. Yes

2. Zero could be shown by a space on the string.

3. a. 687   b. 7,648

Page 16   33

Page 19   15,838

Page 21   4,500,000; about 150,000; about 12,500; about 400

Index